How to be a [Knight]

in 10 easy stages

Written and illustrated by Scoular Anderson

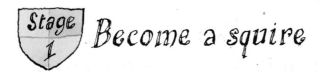

Become a squire

Stage 1

If you'd lived in the **Middle Ages,** you wouldn't have gone to school. Instead, boys and girls from rich families were sent to live with another rich family in their castle or manor.

They learnt how to read, write and play a musical instrument. They learnt good manners and had to serve their lord and lady at mealtimes. Boys were called **pages.** Girls were called ... girls!

At the age of 14, a page became a **squire**. He would learn how to look after his master's horse and keep his armour and weapons in good order.

One day he would go into battle, so he learnt how to fight.

He practised with the longbow.

He used a wooden sword to learn hand-to-hand combat.

He learnt how to hold a lance by running at the **quintain**. If he didn't get out of the way quickly, the sack of sand would swing round and hit him.

3

Make a few promises

When he was 21,
the squire's training was
finished. He was ready
to become a knight.
But first, he had to pray
all night in a church.

The next day, in front of lots of important
people, the young squire knelt before his lord ...

... and made some promises.
This was the Code of **Chivalry**.

A knight must:

be brave...	show courage in battle
be loyal...	obey his lord and fight for him in battle
show mercy...	if his enemy surrenders the knight must spare his life
be generous...	look after his servants and share any plunder he gets in battle
show justice...	be fair in everything he does
be humble...	not boast about things he has done

I dub thee knight!

Arise, Sir Greentree.

Then the lord touched
the squire's shoulders
with a sword.

5

Stage 3 — Get some armour

Every knight needed a suit of armour to protect himself in battle. The armour was made of metal plates shaped to fit his body. They were tied together with leather straps so he could move easily.

a jacket and hood made of chain mail – little rings of metal hooked together

breastplate

padded jerkin

gauntlet

cuisse
(thigh protector)

greave
(leg protector)

spurs

The knight would put on his helmet
last, because during battle it got hot
and sweaty inside.

Some knights decorated
their helmets with
feathers or cloth.

visor – this
could be lifted
up to show the face

← eye-holes

breathing holes

He carried a shield
made of wood and
covered with leather.

The knight needed several weapons for a battle.

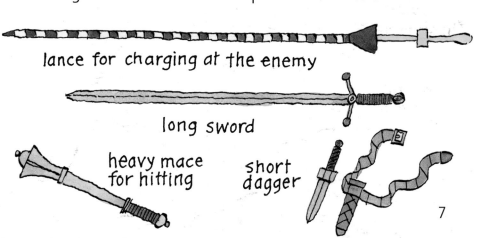

lance for charging at the enemy

long sword

heavy mace
for hitting

short
dagger

Choose your horse

A horse was very expensive to buy and look after.
A knight usually needed three horses.

Charger: a big heavy horse to ride in battle. It had to be able to stop and turn quickly.

Palfrey: a small horse to move slowly and smoothly. A knight needed a gentle ride over long distances – especially if he was wounded in battle.

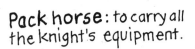

Pack horse: to carry all the knight's equipment.

Before the Middle Ages, soldiers rode on small, swift horses. But it was hard to fight on the back of a horse without falling off.

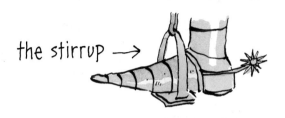

the stirrup →

Stirrups were invented to hold knights' feet in place. This meant a knight could stand up and use his lance or sword with great force.

Before   After   9

Design your coat of arms

In battle, knights wore
helmets which covered
their faces. Every knight had
his own pattern or picture
on his shield, clothes or
flag so he could be easily
recognised. This was called
his coat-of-arms.

A herald had to make
sure that no knight had
the same coat-of-arms
as another.

Heralds kept a list of all the coats-of-arms. This was called Heraldry. Heraldry used unusual names for the colours on shields.

Heraldry used seven colours.

or (gold)   argent (silver)   sable (black)   gules (red)   azure (blue)   vert (green)   purpure (purple)

You could divide your shield with lines.

fesse   pale   chevron   ordee   pall

You could put any picture on your shield.
Dragons, lions and eagles were popular.

Get a big house

Most knights lived in **manor** houses.
Richer, more powerful knights were called
lords and they usually lived in castles.

← manor house

moat

gatehouse
with guard
room upstairs

portcullis (gate which
could be lowered)

drawbridge (which
could be raised)

moat

castle

great hall where the lord ate and entertained guests

sleeping quarters for lord and family

main door

kitchen and store rooms

smaller buildings in the courtyard like stables

battlements

outer walls

13

 Let the lady take charge

When the knight was away fighting, his wife was in charge. She looked after his lands, farms, money and servants. If troublemakers came to the castle, she organized servants and weapons to protect their home.

When the knight returned she put on a feast.

Menu

bread

chicken stuffed with grapes

cheese flan

fish flavoured with herbs

buttered vegetables

roast peacock

jelly

wine and beer

14

For the feast, the guests put on smart clothes and were on their best behaviour. Many books were written about table manners.

At the table

- do not eat with dirty nails
- do not gnaw bones
- do not blow on soup to cool it
- do not pick your teeth with your knife
- do not wipe your mouth with the tablecloth
- do not spit or burp
- do not scratch your flea bites

During the meal, there'd be music and fun.
There might be acrobats, and a jester to tell jokes.

15

Have some fun

A knight wasn't always fighting battles.
Now and then he could relax at home.

He might play
a game of chess.

He might make toys
for his children.

He might enjoy
some music.

16

A knight and his wife often went hunting
or hawking. They rode into the countryside
to hunt deer. In winter, they used hawks to hunt
for rabbits and hares.

If the weather was fine, they might have
a barbecue in the woods.

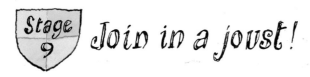

Stage 9 Join in a joust!

Jousts were competitions where knights could show off their fighting skills. They were bright and lively events.

judges' box

arming **pavilions** where the knights prepared for the joust

heralds

trumpeters

pages ready with spare weapons

There were three sorts of joust:

with lances:	two knights charge at each other on horseback
on foot:	two knights fight with swords
the melée:	teams of knights fight a battle

box for important guests

lady of the joust - she presented prizes to the winners

the list (wooden barrier)

double fence and **marshals** to stop supporters running onto the field

Win a battle

In battle, knights charged at the enemy together. It was difficult to stop a group of knights on horseback. But if a knight fell off his horse he was in danger. An enemy soldier could push a weapon through a space between his armour.

Equipment used during a siege

boiling oil poured down on attackers

mangonel- giant catapult which hurled rocks

battering ram- to break down castle gate

If the enemy was inside a castle, the knights had to organize a **siege** outside. They would surround the castle with men and weapons. If the enemy didn't surrender, the knights and their men attacked.

belfry-tower which let soldiers reach the top of the castle walls

caltrops - little spikes thrown on the ground that stuck in soldiers' feet or horses' hooves

mine-tunnel dug under the castle wall so it would collapse

ladders

You had to be brave to be a knight. You also had to be rich! So, do you think you want to be a knight?

Glossary

chivalry	helping and respecting everyone
jousts	competitions between two knights on horseback
manor	a large country house
marshals	people who keep order during sports matches
Middle Ages	the years between 1000 and 1499
moat	a trench around a castle, usually filled with water

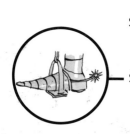

pages	boys who are training to become squires
pavilions	large tents
quintain	a practice shield on a wooden pole
siege	surrounding a castle and starving the people inside
squire	a young man who is training to be a knight
stirrups	metal loops to keep a horse rider's feet in place

Index

Ideas for guided reading

Learning objectives: tell real and imagined stories using the conventions of familiar story language; read independently and with increasing fluency longer and less familiar texts; draw together information and ideas from across the whole text, using simple signposts; explain their reactions to texts, commenting on important aspects; maintain consistency in non narrative, including purpose and tense

Curriculum links: History: Knowledge and understanding of events, people and changes in the past

Interest words: chivalry, quintain, herald, jousts, manor, marshals, Middle Ages, moat, pages, pavilions, siege, squire, stirrups, visor

Resources: drawing materials

Word count: 993

Getting started

- Ask the children to read the covers and leaf through the book deciding what kind of book this is and what it might tell us.

- Demonstrate reading pp2–3 and discuss new words such as *squire* and *quintain*. Model how to use the glossary to check the meanings of these words.

- Discuss the layout. *Are the drawings helpful? Is the language interesting? Is the book easy to understand? How could we use the chapter headings?*

- Return to the contents page, and give each child a chapter to read independently, explaining that they will have to report back to the group on what they have found out.

Reading and responding

- Listen to each child read in turn as the others read independently.

- Encourage the children to use phonic decoding strategies to read any unfamiliar words they might meet. Use context to decide what these words mean.